my *Missouri* garden

a gardener's journal

my Missouri garden

a gardener's journal

Mike Miller

COOL SPRINGS PRESS

ISBN 1-930604-08-4

NOTE: The ideas expressed in this book are not, in all cases, exact quotations, as some have been edited to fit the format. In all cases, the publisher has attempted to maintain the speaker's original intent. Further, in some cases, source materials for this book were obtained from secondary sources, primarily print media and the Internet. While every effort has been made to ensure the accuracy of these sources, accuracy cannot be guaranteed. To notify us of any corrections or clarifications, please contact Cool Springs Press.

Cool Springs Press, Inc.
112 Second Avenue North
Franklin, TN 37064

First Printing 2000
Printed in the United States of America
10 9 8 7 6 5 4 3 2 1

Design by: Sheri Ferguson
Illustrations by: Allison Starcher
Editorial Consultant: Erica Glasener

this is my

Missouri

garden

---

name

---

year

why keep a garden journal ?

Welcome! We Missourians live in a state rich in natural beauty. Anyone who sets out to establish a healthy and beautiful landscape will discover gardening is a constant learning process. That's why you will enjoy *My Missouri Garden: A Gardener's Journal*.

Keeping a garden journal will help you keep track of how your garden grows. You will discover which plants thrive, which ones struggle, and best of all, you will discover many surprises. More than just record keeping, journaling is a way to trace your growth as a gardener. Writing down your favorite moments in the garden may help you decide which plants to add or which to replace. How does your garden make you feel? Maybe your style of gardening has changed. A journal will help you track the evolution of your garden.

As gardeners know, weather is a huge factor in plant performance. By keeping track of air temperature, the amount of rainfall, and drastic changes (storms or droughts), we can see which plants survived and plan better for next year.

Has the environment in your garden changed? Trees and shrubs that were once small may have matured and created a shadier garden. Keeping a list of what you plant, where and when you plant it, and the source of the plant will provide useful information for the future.

Further, keeping up with what's blooming when, and how long it blooms is another reason to write daily or weekly in a garden journal. You might be surprised at how many seasons your garden features beautiful blooms, colorful foliage, or fantastic fruits. Some of the best color combinations happen by accident and remembering which plant blooms and when it blooms from year to year is not easy. But with good journal records, you may recreate pleasing plant combinations and avoid repeating mistakes.

How often you fertilize, prune, and water are other things to keep track of in your garden journal. Which techniques have been most successful? If you have a particular pest or disease problem with one plant, what methods were effective in eradicating or controlling the problem? If your roses were beautiful last year, when did you prune them and how much did you prune? When did you divide your phlox and where did you plant the different varieties of spring bulbs? All of these questions can be answered in the pages of *My Missouri Garden*.

getting started with your garden journal

By keeping daily records, you can check your journal and chart your most successful garden practices. Whether it's how and when you propagated a favorite hydrangea or rose, when the first iris came into bloom, or when you noticed the scent of a particular native azalea, your Missouri garden journal will provide the ideal format for keeping in touch with your garden and what it can teach you. Here's how to get started.

- Designate a day and a time during the week to write in your journal. You might discover that early morning coffee time or the end of the day works best.
- Use a favorite pen and keep it with your journal. Write brief, clear notes (*rainy and cool with temp around 60° F, Phlox 'David' has been in bloom for 2 weeks, Vitex loaded with flower buds, planted two hardy geraniums in perennial garden, 'Johnson's Blue', and 'Claridge Druce', purchased from the specialty nursery in Oregon*).
- Keep a 5" x 7" envelope tucked in the back of your journal to hold photographs and pictures from catalogs or magazines that inspire you. Be sure to identify and label pictures.
- List existing trees, shrubs, perennials, and bulbs, including a sketch of where they are located. This will be especially helpful over the years when you make changes in your garden.

Once you get used to journaling, you may find that you look forward to writing about your garden as much as you enjoy adding new plants.

{ introduction }

Learning all of the special information that makes a landscape unique is both a challenge and a joy that will bring many enduring rewards in the long and healthy lives of your plants.

Study the environmental conditions in your garden and let the garden tell you what to do. Familiarize yourself with the native or common plants of your region and use them as a guide to selections for your garden, both native and exotic. Knowing the type of soil, light, and exposure your plants require will help you select the right plant for the right place. You will probably want to select plants that tolerate your landscape's climate to increase survival and minimize maintenance. With the exception of large trees and shrubs, don't be afraid to move your plants. Often conditions change, and what was once a favorable environment may no longer be. Proper watering, mulch, and fertilizer further help to ensure the success of your garden.

the plan

It can be useful to consult a professional garden designer or landscape architect to help you plan your garden. Their work can be as detailed as a drawing with every plant sited or as broad as a simple list of recommended plants for particular areas. If you have just moved into your house, observe the garden one whole growing season before you hire someone to help you develop a plan. This experience will help you determine which areas receive the most light and which are in shade, etc. Once you have a plan, you can implement it in stages over time. Making adjustments as conditions or your tastes change is easy. You may also refer to my book, *Missouri Gardener's Guide* (Cool Springs Press, 1998), for specific plant recommendations and advice for Missouri gardeners.

soil

Soil is the foundation of our landscape. Experienced gardeners become connoisseurs of soil. We do a careful site evaluation to determine the specific soil structure, the nutrient and organic levels, the pH (relative chemical) level, and the nature of the landscape's subterranean insect and animal life.

Soil is a living and ever-changing environment, and mastering it is a matter of learning how the climatic factors affect the soil, how it is changed by plant root growth, by the seasonal loss of leaves, needles, and flowers, and by animal and insect activity. It is important to know what type of soil you have in order to garden successfully.

amending your soil

Compost is one of the best soil amendments because it is alive with billions of creatures to help roots absorb water and nutrients. Decomposed leaves, lawn clippings, pruned branches, and discarded plant parts harbor the fungi, bacteria, and other living creatures that are important parts of healthy soil.

Making compost can be as simple as piling leaves and clippings in a heap and letting them break down. You can add kitchen waste such as coffee grounds, clean eggshells, and uncooked vegetable scraps to your compost pile. It is best not to add animal fats, bones, or meat.

Be patient! It will take approximately six months and a 30-gallon bag of yard trimmings to yield 1 cubic foot of compost from your pile.

Although peat moss is readily available, it breaks down too quickly. The best organic matter is found in manure, compost, and other materials. For best results, mix organic matter into a depth of 6-8 inches. Work the soil when it is dry to avoid clods forming when the soil gets wet. This will also result in a more even mixture.

soil test

A soil test helps determine how much fertilizer to apply and whether any additives (such as lime) are needed. A soil sample can be professionally tested to discover the levels of all the soil's components, and this information can be used to make needed modifications. Because of Missouri's extremes of climate, complete soil preparation is recommended.

Contact your Missouri Extension Office. Personnel there can provide you with the necessary forms and information for soil testing, or you can contact a state-certified, soil-testing laboratory. Soil acidity is measured in numbers from 1 to 14 on the pH scale. Most plants prefer a soil that has a pH of 6.5 to 7. The soil test report will tell you how much and what type of fertilizer or other additives to use for the type of plant you are growing, the soil pH and what, if anything, should be done to protect it.

nutrients

The main nutrients plants need are nitrogen, phosphorous, and potassium. When you buy fertilizer you will see 3 numbers on the bag representing the percentage of each nutrient in the mixture. For example, a bag of 10-10-10 fertilizer contains 10% nitrogen (N), 10% phosphorus (P), and 10% potassium (K). The other 70% is filler such as clay.

Each nutrient serves a function in the overall good health of a plant. Nitrogen promotes leaf growth. That is why lawn fertilizer has a high nitrogen percentage. Phosphorous is important in the formation of roots as well as flower, seed, and fruit growth. That is why starter fertilizers and bloom fertilizers have high percentages of phosphorous. Potassium increases overall cell health. When plants are under stress from drought or cold, adequate potassium helps the plant withstand the crisis.

mulch

Mulch acts like a blanket, holding moisture in the soil and keeping the soil temperature from getting too hot or cold. Mulch can also help reduce weed infestations.

tips when mulching:

- Apply a 1- to 2-inch layer of mulch on top of the soil around all plants. At the same time, avoid piling mulch against the trunks or stems of plants. This could lead to potential disease problems.
- Pine straw, wood chips, and shredded leaves are good choices.

watering

Watering seems like a simple thing, but gardeners have a tendency to overwater or underwater plants. Sandy soils drain quickly, requiring watering at least twice a week during blistering summers. Clay soils hold water, therefore plants growing in clay need less watering.

guidelines for watering:

- Water your container plants until the water runs out the bottom. During hot summer months some containers may need water twice a day. Do not water until the top inch of the soil is dry to the touch.

- Put a hose at the base of a newly installed tree or shrub and thoroughly soak the rootball weekly. As the plant grows, the area that needs to be soaked will increase as the root zone increases.
- Use shallow cans (tuna, etc.) to measure the amount of water applied by your lawn sprinkler. Put six cans in the area you are watering and run the system for an hour. Then measure the depth of the water in all cans. When the average depth of the water is $1/2$ inch, the grass root zone has been irrigated. This may take one to two hours.
- Buy an inexpensive water timer and a few soaker hoses. They are a worthwhile investment. During periods of drought, mature trees will benefit from long, slow watering.

get started journaling and have fun

Your garden is what you make it. If you keep your heart and mind open to the nuances of nature, you will cultivate more than just pretty flowers and strong trees. Both you and your plants will grow in your beautiful garden. Hopefully, you will also have fun creating lovely gardens. May you experience many enjoyable gardening hours!

Missouri Garden Favorites

Here in Missouri, we are blessed with such plant variety that there are delightful selections for each month of the year. I have found the following choices to be great performers because they are easy to grow, readily available, adaptable to various growing conditions, and help provide year-round interest. These plants can be very beneficial to your Missouri garden because they provide brilliant color, some attract birds and wildlife, and most require minimal maintenance. You will find most of my recommendations in my book *Missouri Gardener's Guide* (Cool Springs Press, 1998). Give these a try!

January

- English Ivy — *Hedera helix*
- Maiden Grass — *Miscanthus sinensis* 'Gracillimus'
- Upright Keteleeri Juniper — *Juniperus chinensis* 'Keteleeri'
- River Birch — *Betula nigra*
- Winter Creeper — *Euonymus fortunei* 'Colorata'
- Red Twig Dogwood — *Cornus sericea* 'Kelsey'

February

- Winter Aconite — *Eranthis hyemalis*
- Dutch White Clover — *Trifolium repens*
- Pussy or Goat Willow — *Salix caprea*
- Inkberry Holly— *Ilex glabra*
- Serbian Spruce — *Picea omorika*
- European Beech Tree — *Fagus sylvatica*
- Iris — *Iris* spp.
- Boston Ivy — *Parthenocissus tricuspidata*

March

- Snowdrops — *Galanthus nivalis*
- Kentucky Bluegrass — *Poa pratensis*
- Spring Witch Hazel — *Hamamelis vernalis*
- Spiderwort — *Tradescantia virginiana*
- Solomons Seal — *Polygonatum commutatum*
- Blue Bells — *Mertensia virginica*
- Amur Maple — *Acer ginnala*
- Upright Yew — *Taxus* x *media* 'Hicksii'

April

- Creeping Phlox — *Phlox subulata*
- Serviceberry — *Amelanchier arborea*
- Crocus — *Crocus* spp.
- Arrowwood Viburnum — *Viburnum dentatum*
- Redbud — *Cercis canadensis*
- Daffodils — *Narcissus* spp.
- Grape Hyacinth — *Muscari* spp.
- Snowflake — *Leucojum aestivum*
- Tulip — *Tulipa* spp.

May

- Celadine Poppy — *Stylorphorum diphyllum*
- Bishop's Weed — *Aegopodium podagraria* 'Picta'
- Peony — *Paeonia lactiflora*
- Dogwood — *Cornus flordia* 'Cherokee Princess'
- Lily-of-the-Valley — *Convallaria majalis*
- Columbine — *Aquilegia canadensis*
- Tulip Tree — *Liriodendron tulipfera*

June

- Chinese Dogwood — *Cornus kousa*
- Climbing Zephrine Drouhin — *Rosa* 'Zephrine Drouhin'
- Europeana Rose — *Rosa* 'Europeana'
- Tricolor Beech — *Fagus sylvatica* 'Purpurea Tricolor'
- Bugle Weed — *Ajuga reptans*
- Snowball Bush — *Hydrangea arborescens* 'Annabelle'
- Begonia — *Begonia* x *semperflorens-cultorum*

July

- Red Japanese Maple — *Acer palmatum* 'Bloodgood'
- Hosta — *Hosta fortunei*
- Zoysia — *Zoysia japonica*
- Astilbe — *Astilbe* x *arendsii*
- Summersweet — *Clethra alnifolia*
- Cardinal Climber — *Quanmoclit sloteri*
- Hyacinth Bean — *Lablab purpureus*
- Goat's Beard — *Aruncus dioicus*
- Impatiens — *Impatiens wallerana*

August

- Gladiolus — *Gladiolus* x *hortulanum*
- Tall Phlox — *Phlox paniculata*
- Red Barberry — *Berberis thungergii* var. *atropurpurea*
- Tickseed — *Coreopsis verticillata* 'Zagreb'
- Butterfly Plant — *Asclepias tuberosa*
- Improved Flowering Pear — *Pyrus calleryana* 'Aristocrat'
- Purple Coneflower — *Echinacea purpurea*
- Morning Glory — *Ipomoea tricolor*

September

- Cockscomb — *Celosia cristata*
- Caladium — *Caladium* x *hortulanum*
- Balsam — *Impatiens balsamisa*
- The Fairy Rose — *Rosa* 'The Fairy'
- Fall Windflower — *Anemone* x *hybrida*
- Blue Sage — *Salvia farinacea*
- Trumpet Vine — *Campsis radicans*
- Liveforever — *Hylotelephium spectabile*

October

- Red Fountain Grass — *Pennisetum setaceum* 'Rubrum'
- Globe Amaranth — *Gomphrene globosa*
- Black Gum — *Nyssa sylvatica*
- Dahlia — *Dahlia* hybrids
- Donald Wyman Crabapple — *Malus* 'Donald Wyman'
- Red Sunset Maple — *Acer rubrum* 'Red Sunset'
- French Marigold — *Tagetes patula*
- Canna — *Canna* x *generalis*
- Fringetree — *Chionanthus virginicus*
- Yarrow — *Achillea millefolium*

November

- Blue Lyme Grass — *Leymis arenarius*
- Bittersweet Vine — *Celastrus scandens*
- Deciduous Winterberry Holly — *Ilex verticillata* 'Winter Red'
- Globe Arborvitae — *Thuja occidentalis* 'Woodwardi'
- Bald Cypress — *Taxodium distichum*
- Silver Lace Vine — *Fallopia baldschuanica*
- Giant Reed Grass — *Arundo donax*
- Rose Verbena — *Verbena Canadensis*
- Sneezeweed — *Helenium autumnale*

December

- Stone Crop — *Sedum spurium* 'Dragon's Blood'
- Washington Hawthorn — *Crataegus phaenopyrum*
- Fountain Grass — *Pennisetum setaceum*
- Hemlock — *Tsuga Canadensis*
- Pansy — *Viola* x *wittrockiana*
- Red Oak — *Quercus rubra*
- Norway Spruce — *Picea abies*
- Scarlet Meidiland — *Rosa* 'Keitoli' or 'Meikrotal'
- Bayberry — *Myrica pensylvanica*

{ missouri hardiness zone map }

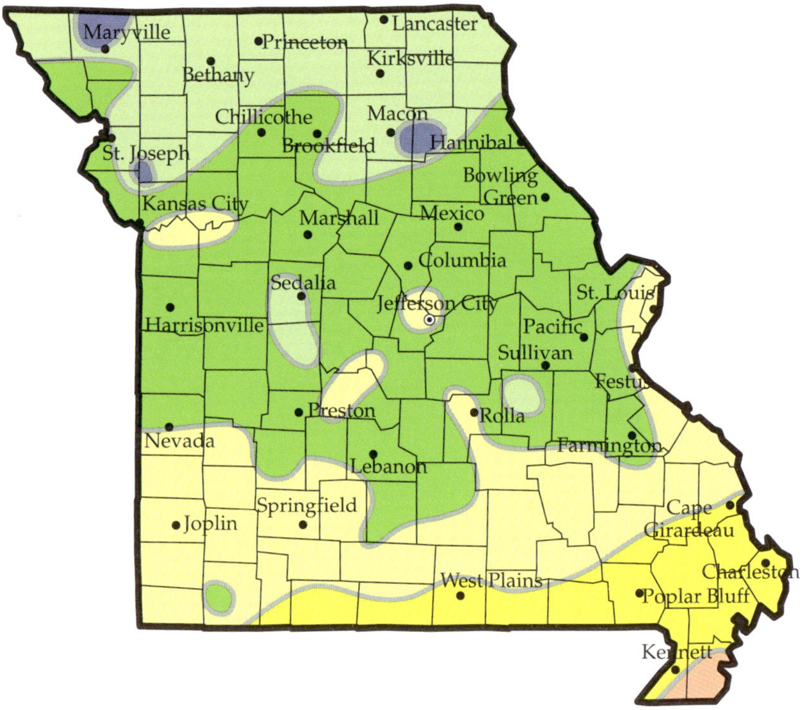

Average Annual Minimum Temperature

4B	-20° F to -25° F
5A	-15° F to -20° F
5B	-10° F to -15° F
6A	-5° F to -10° F
6B	0° F to -5° F
7A	5° F to 0° F

To create a
little flower is the
labour of ages.

— William Blake

january | week 1

January

garden observations

what's the weather like?

Start the year off right! Photograph your garden at least once every month. This will help you with your planning and planting schemes.

what have I planted/transplanted?

garden notes

What is a weed? A plant whose virtues have not yet been dicovered.

—Ralph Waldo Emerson

january | week 2

January

garden observations

Order seeds now for your favorite annuals, perennials and vegetables. Cut out color photographs and create your own record for what you order.

what's the weather like?

When planning your garden, use a large sheet of graph paper with 1/4 inch grids. A scale of 1 inch = 4 feet is a useful proportion.

what have I planted/transplanted?

garden notes

January

garden observations

what's the weather like?

what have I planted/transplanted?

garden notes

Check house plants for signs of insects and disease. Spots, speckles or webs on leaves indicate pests are present.

January

garden observations

what's the weather like?

Tip to Remember: You may also use vegetables as ornamental plants. Ornamental peppers and sweet potato vine selections are good examples.

what have I planted/transplanted?

garden notes

february | week 1

garden observations

what's the weather like?

what have I planted/transplanted?

Take a walk through your garden, and plan additions to create winter interest for next year.

Did You Know?
The only tulip color that has not yet been developed is any shade of blue.

garden notes

garden observations

what's the weather like?

When in doubt, call your local Extension Service. Master Gardeners there will provide information (and the advice is free!)

what have I planted/transplanted?

garden notes

february | week 3

February

garden observations

Extend the life of your cut flowers. Remove the lower leaves and re-cut the stems before arranging them in lukewarm water.

what's the weather like?

what have I planted/transplanted?

garden notes

Though I do not believe that a plant will spring up where no seed has been, I have great faith in a seed. Convince me that you have a seed there, and I am prepared to expect wonders.

—Henry David Thoreau

february | week 4

garden observations

what's the weather like?

Tip to Remember:
Fill clear plastic milk jugs with water and place around young tomato plants. They will provide warmth overnight for young plants, helping you get a jump on spring.

what have I planted/transplanted?

garden notes

march week 1

March

what's blooming?

Direct sow wildflower seeds where you want them to grow in climates with USDA zones 1 through 6. (Check the zone map in the introduction to identify your zone.)

what's the weather like?

Take a soil test now so you will know how to prepare your garden for the next season.

what have I planted/transplanted?

garden notes

March

what's blooming?

Tip to Remember:
Plan to add a few annuals to your perennial garden to help provide season-long blooms.

what's the weather like?

Watch for aphids on shrubs as they leaf out. Treat with insecticidal soap or any other labeled pesticide, if needed.

what have I planted/transplanted?

Start tomato seeds for transplants 4-6 weeks before optimum planting time in your area.

garden notes

march | week 3

March

what's blooming?

Single-flower forms of marigolds and zinnias are more appealing to butterflies than the double-flower forms.

what's the weather like?

Did You Know? Viburnum is a member of the honeysuckle family.

what have I planted/transplanted?

garden notes

march | week 4

March

what's blooming?

what's the weather like?

Hummingbirds love tubular flowers such as trumpet vine, coral honeysuckle, and nicotiana. Plant lots of these if you want to attract hummingbirds.

what have I planted/transplanted?

garden notes

Half the interest of a garden is the constant exercise of the imagination.

— C.W. Earle

april | week 1

what's blooming?

what's the weather like?

what have I planted/transplanted?

Have you photographed your garden lately? This will help with your garden planning and design ideas.

An easy time to weed is the day after a gentle rain, when the soil is slightly moist, and weeds are easy to pull—roots and all.

garden notes

april week 2

what's blooming?

what's the weather like?

what have I planted/transplanted?

Propagate some of your favorite broadleaf shrubs using this simple layering technique: Select a branch that is close to the ground. Bend the branch so that it is in contact with the soil. Cover the branch with soil. Water well and hold the branch in place with a brick. In six weeks, check to see if there are roots. Once the roots are firmly established, cut the new plant off from the mother plant.

garden notes

As is the gardener, such is the garden.

—Hebrew Proverb

april week 3

what's blooming?

Tip to Remember: When digging a hole for a tree, it's best to dig the hole at least half again as wide as the size of the rootball (much wider is even better). Use the same soil you dug out to backfill around the rootball and water-in well.

what's the weather like?

Turn your compost pile. If you haven't started one already, call your Extension Service for advice.

what have I planted/transplanted?

garden notes

april | week 4

what's blooming?

what's the weather like?

Wooden clothespins can be used as plant markers.

Place grow-thru stakes above plants that need support in early spring, and in a short time they will cover the stakes.

what have I planted/transplanted?

garden notes

may week 1

May

Plan to prune back spring-blooming azaleas and other shrubs such as forsythia or spirea after they finish flowering. This way you won't cut off any potential flower buds for next year.

what's blooming?

Check plants once or twice a week for insect and disease problems. It's easier to control a small infestation if it's discovered early.

what's the weather like?

what have I planted/transplanted?

garden notes

may week 2

what's blooming?

what's the weather like?

what have I planted/transplanted?

Incorporate a slow-release fertilizer in the soil of hanging baskets and container plantings. This will provide nutrients for several months in one application.

garden notes

Many diseases can be controlled with sanitation. Remove and destroy any infected leaves as soon as they are found.

may week 3

what's blooming?

what's the weather like?

Parsley and fennel provide food for butterfly caterpillars.

Interest children in gardening by planning a small child's garden. A bean tee-pee is fun to plant and grow!

what have I planted/transplanted?

garden notes

The best time for slug hunting is at night using a flashlight and a pair of gloves.

may | week 4

Did You Know?

Bees are our most efficient pollinators for flowers, fruits, and vegetables. Any garden with lots of bees is a healthy environment.

what's blooming?

what's the weather like?

what have I planted/transplanted?

garden notes

Tickle it with a hoe and it will laugh into a harvest.

—English Proverb

june week 1

A perennial garden looks wonderful when planted against a background of a wall, a hedge, or evergreen shrubs.

A plant's scientific name consists of a genus and an epithet. The genus and the epithet are always italicized and the genus begins with a capital letter. A third word in the name may refer to a specific variety, called a cultivar. It is set off by single quotation marks.

what's blooming?

what's the weather like?

what have I planted/transplanted?

garden notes

june week 2

June

what's blooming?

Use vines to create vertical interest in the garden. If you don't have a wall or fence on which to train them, a lattice or arbor will work.

what's the weather like?

You can create your own portable seep irrigation system by punching a few holes in plastic containers and placing them beside plants that need additional moisture.

what have I planted/transplanted?

garden notes

Though an old man,
I am but a young
gardener...

—Thomas Jefferson

june week 3

June

Plan to shear fall-blooming asters to make them bushier and more compact.

what's blooming?

what's the weather like?

what have I planted/transplanted?

Did You Know?

Even though a plant may be identified as self-cleaning, flowers are better off if you deadhead, or remove the spent blooms as often as you can. This will allow the plant to use its energy to make more flowers and leaves instead of making seeds.

garden notes

june week 4

what's blooming?

what's the weather like?

BTK (*Bacillus thuringiensis kurstaki*) is an organic biological control that is effective against many caterpillars and is safe to use on vegetable crops. *Bacillus thuringiensis* 'San Diego' is effective against some leafeating beetles.

what have I planted/transplanted?

garden notes

tending my garden

june | week 4

july week 1

Harvest herbs for drying as soon as they come into flower. Bundle them up with a rubber band and hang them on a line in a dark, dry place with good air circulation. To preserve the best flavor once they are dry, store the herbs in airtight containers away from heat and light.

Press some flowers and add to this journal. It's a pretty record of what you planted.

what's blooming?

what's the weather like?

what have I planted/transplanted?

garden notes

july | week 2

what's blooming?

what's the weather like?

what have I planted/transplanted?

Deadhead hybrid tea roses throughout the summer to encourage more blooms.

garden notes

july week 3

what's blooming?

what's the weather like?

Most unwanted summer heat comes through east- and west-facing windows, not through well-insulated roofs and walls. Plant a deciduous tree for shade.

what have I planted/transplanted?

garden notes

july week 4

what's blooming?

Plants use calcium to build strong cell walls and stems. Deficiencies can cause blossom-end rot on tomatoes.

what's the weather like?

Did You Know? The Greeks and Romans used lavender in bath water. In fact, the Latin name "lavare" means, "wash".

Tip to Remember: When planting seeds, position them in geometric patterns so that you will be able to distinguish them more easily from weed seedlings.

what have I planted/transplanted?

garden notes

Gardening is the purest of human pleasures.

—Francis Bacon

august week 1

what's blooming?

what's the weather like?

Preserve basil leaves by mixing them in the blender with a small amount of water. Fill ice cube trays with the mixture. Once they freeze, put them in freezer bags. This way you will have basil to use in your favorite Italian dishes all winter long.

what have I planted/transplanted?

garden notes

august | week 2

August

what's blooming?

For the best selection, order your spring-flowering bulbs or purchase them locally when they become available in your area. Keep them cool and dry until you plant them.

what's the weather like?

Take some photographs of your garden to refer to later when planning for next year.

what have I planted/transplanted?

garden notes

august week 3

If you haven't already done so, draw a plan of your property showing existing trees and shrubs in relation to your house. Make notes throughout the year indicating those areas that receive full sun, shade or a mix of sun and shade. This will help you to choose the right plant for the right place.

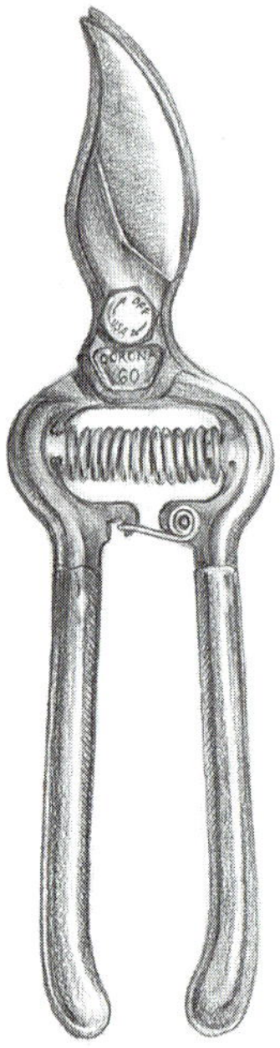

what's blooming?

what's the weather like?

what have I planted/transplanted?

garden notes

august week 4

August

what's blooming?

Water your compost pile when the weather has been dry.

what's the weather like?

Order three or four types of paperwhite narcissus to force at two-week intervals. You will have flowers from Halloween into the New Year!

what have I planted/transplanted?

Continue to harvest vegetables as soon as they are ripe. Regular harvesting increases production.

garden notes

He who plants a garden plants happiness.

—Chinese Proverb

september | week 1

what's blooming?

what's the weather like?

Expand your plant collection by exchanging seeds and plants with fellow gardeners.

what have I planted/transplanted?

Add some shrubs to your garden that will offer winter interest such as colorful bark, or unusual shapes.

garden notes

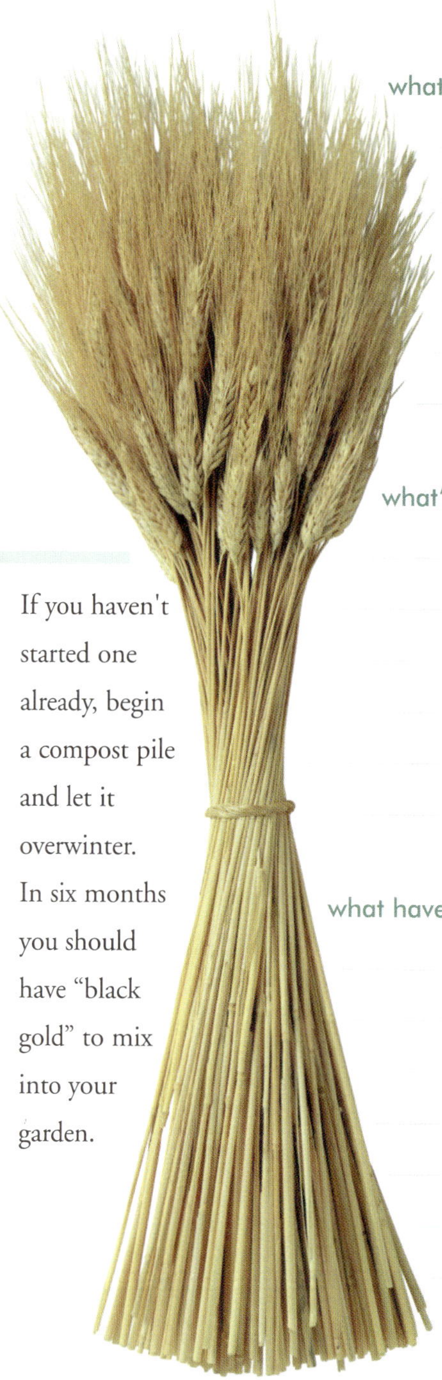

what's blooming?

what's the weather like?

If you haven't started one already, begin a compost pile and let it overwinter. In six months you should have "black gold" to mix into your garden.

what have I planted/transplanted?

garden notes

The frost hurts not weeds.

—Thomas Fuller

september | week 3

what's blooming?

what's the weather like?

what have I planted/transplanted?

garden notes

If your annuals are beginning to look ragged, pull them and replace with some mums, pansies, or flowering kale.

september | week 4

what's blooming?

Use dried seed heads such as sedum and lotus for fall decorations.

Visit your favorite nursery to select a tree or shrub for that spot in the garden that needs something new.

what's the weather like?

what have I planted/transplanted?

garden notes

october | week 1

what's blooming?

what's the weather like?

Plant a tree in honor of a birth or in memory of a loved one.

Fall leaf color is triggered by cooler temperatures, shorter days, and less light.

what have I planted/transplanted?

garden notes

october | week 2

October

what's blooming?

what's the weather like?

what have I planted/transplanted?

garden notes

Sprinkle annual rye grass seed on top of the soil of pots you are forcing. By the time the bulbs bloom, it will create a green carpet underneath them.

october | week 3

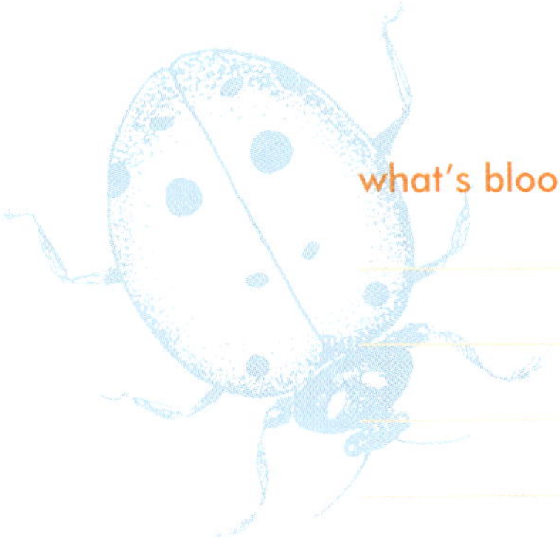

what's blooming?

what's the weather like?

Tip to Remember: Parsley is a good plant for bed edges. It also looks great grown in containers with pansies.

what have I planted/transplanted?

Use golf tees to mark areas where bulbs are planted.

garden notes

Heaven is under our feet as well as over our heads.

—Henry David Thoreau

october | week 4

what's blooming?

what's the weather like?

Did You Know?
The word 'wort',
as in St. John's Wort,
is an old English
term that means
"medicinal plant".

what have I planted/transplanted?

garden notes

november | week 1

what's blooming?

what's the weather like?

Fall is the best time to direct sow wildflower seeds in USDA zones 7-9. (Check the map in the introduction to verify your zone.)

what have I planted/transplanted?

garden notes

Autumn is a second spring when every leaf is a flower. —Albert Camus

what's blooming?

what's the weather like?

Continue to mow your lawn for as long as it keeps growing.

Clean and sharpen garden tools. Lightly coat with oil to prevent rust.

what have I planted/transplanted?

garden notes

what's blooming?

what's the weather like?

what have I planted/transplanted?

garden notes

Extend the life of your fresh-cut holiday tree by storing it in a cool shady place until you move it indoors. Re-cut the trunk before moving it indoors and use plenty of fresh water in the reservoir.

november | week 4

what's blooming?

For best results, store unused seeds in a cool, dark place in an air- and water-resistant container.

what's the weather like?

Selecting the right tool for the job can prevent most injuries. Wear safety gear when operating power equipment.

what have I planted/transplanted?

garden notes

december week 1

December

garden observations

Make a wreath for the holidays. Rose hips, bittersweet, and euonymus are good choices for materials.

what's the weather like?

what have I planted/ transplanted?

garden notes

A garden is a friend
you can visit any time.

—unknown

december | week 2

December

garden observations

Cast iron plant, Chinese evergreen, heartleaf philoden-dron, and snake plant will tolerate low-light conditions.

what's the weather like?

Tip to Remember: The winter sun provides the most solar heat through south-facing windows. Avoid planting shade trees or evergreens that may shade these heat-absorbing windows if you need the extra warmth.

what have I planted/transplanted?

garden notes

december week 3

garden observations

Recycle your holiday tree. The branches can be removed and used as mulch. Or you can leave the tree intact and use it as a windbreak and shelter for birds.

Don't put wood ashes in your compost pile; they will alter the pH level too much.

what's the weather like?

what have I planted/transplanted?

garden notes

december | week 4

garden observations

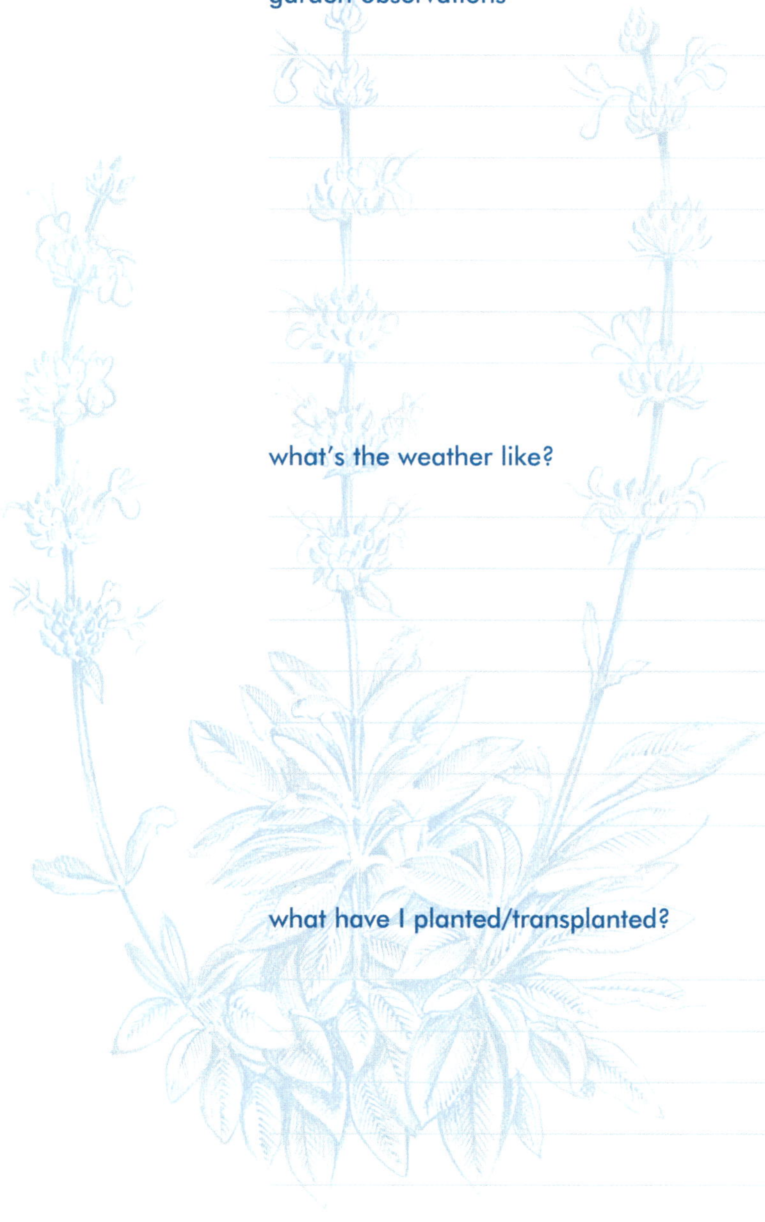

what's the weather like?

what have I planted/transplanted?

Pruning large trees, especially those located near utilities should be performed by a professional. Call a certified arborist if you need trees pruned.

plant inventory/history

name
when planted
where planted
size
source
price

name
when planted
where planted
size
source
price

name
when planted
where planted
size
source
price

name
when planted
where planted
size
source
price

name
when planted
where planted
size
source
price

name
when planted
where planted
size
source
price

name
when planted
where planted
size
source
price

name
when planted
where planted
size
source
price

name
when planted
where planted
size
source
price

name
when planted
where planted
size
source
price

name
when planted
where planted
size
source
price

name
when planted
where planted
size
source
price

name
when planted
where planted
size
source
price

name
when planted
where planted
size
source
price

name
when planted
where planted
size
source
price

name
when planted
where planted
size
source
price

plant inventory/history

name
when planted
where planted
size
source
price

name
when planted
where planted
size
source
price

name
when planted
where planted
size
source
price

name
when planted
where planted
size
source
price

name
when planted
where planted
size
source
price

name
when planted
where planted
size
source
price

name
when planted
where planted
size
source
price

name
when planted
where planted
size
source
price

name

when planted

where planted

size

source

price

name

when planted

where planted

size

source

price

name

when planted

where planted

size

source

price

name

when planted

where planted

size

source

price

name

when planted

where planted

size

source

price

name

when planted

where planted

size

source

price

name

when planted

where planted

size

source

price

name

when planted

where planted

size

source

price

plant inventory/history

name
when planted
where planted
size
source
price

name
when planted
where planted
size
source
price

name
when planted
where planted
size
source
price

name
when planted
where planted
size
source
price

name
when planted
where planted
size
source
price

name
when planted
where planted
size
source
price

name
when planted
where planted
size
source
price

name
when planted
where planted
size
source
price

name
when planted
where planted
size
source
price

name
when planted
where planted
size
source
price

name
when planted
where planted
size
source
price

name
when planted
where planted
size
source
price

name
when planted
where planted
size
source
price

name
when planted
where planted
size
source
price

name
when planted
where planted
size
source
price

name
when planted
where planted
size
source
price

plant inventory/history

name

when planted

where planted

size

source

price

name

when planted

where planted

size

source

price

name

when planted

where planted

size

source

price

name

when planted

where planted

size

source

price

name

when planted

where planted

size

source

price

name

when planted

where planted

size

source

price

name

when planted

where planted

size

source

price

name

when planted

where planted

size

source

price

name | name
when planted | when planted
where planted | where planted
size | size
source | source
price | price

name | name
when planted | when planted
where planted | where planted
size | size
source | source
price | price

name | name
when planted | when planted
where planted | where planted
size | size
source | source
price | price

name | name
when planted | when planted
where planted | where planted
size | size
source | source
price | price

my garden plan

my garden plan

suppliers & resources

photos

photos